Fremdsprachentexte

William Faulkner
Barn Burning

Herausgegeben von
Peter Nicolaisen

W0194620

Philipp Reclam jun. Stuttgart

Diese Ausgabe darf nur in der Bundesrepublik Deutschland, in Österreich und in der Schweiz vertrieben werden.

Universal-Bibliothek Nr. 9043
Alle Rechte vorbehalten
Copyright © für diese Ausgabe 1997 Philipp Reclam jun. GmbH & Co., Stuttgart
Copyright © für den Text 1950 Random House, Inc. »Barn Burning« erschien erstmals 1939 in *Harper's Magazine*. Abdruck mit Genehmigung von Random House, Inc., New York
Gesamtherstellung: Reclam, Ditzingen. Printed in Germany 1997
RECLAM und UNIVERSAL-BIBLIOTHEK sind eingetragene Marken der Philipp Reclam jun. GmbH & Co., Stuttgart
ISBN 3-15-009043-1

Barn Burning

The store in which the Justice of the Peace's court was
sitting smelled of cheese. The boy, crouched on his nail
keg at the back of the crowded room, knew he smelled
5 cheese, and more: from where he sat he could see the
ranked shelves close-packed with the solid, squat, dynamic shapes of tin cans whose labels his stomach read,
not from the lettering which meant nothing to his mind
but from the scarlet devils and the silver curve of fish[1]
10 – this, the cheese which he knew he smelled and the
hermetic meat which his intestines believed he smelled
coming in intermittent gusts momentary and brief between the other constant one, the smell and sense just
a little of fear because mostly of despair and grief, the
15 old fierce pull of blood. He could not see the table
where the Justice sat and before which his father and

---

3 **to crouch:** hocken.
3 f. **nail keg:** kleines Faß mit Nägeln.
6 **ranked:** aufgereiht.
   close-packed: vollgepackt.
   squat: plump.
6 f. **dynamic:** wuchtig.
7 **label:** Etikett.
8 **lettering:** Beschriftung.
11 **hermetic:** luftdicht abgeschlossen, verpackt.
   intestines: Eingeweide, Gedärm.
12 **intermittent:** stoßweise auftretend.
   gust: Schwall, Woge.
   momentary: kurz, flüchtig.

his father's enemy (*our enemy* he thought in that de-spair; *ourn! mine and hisn both! He's my father!*) stood, but he could hear them, the two of them that is, be-cause his father had said no word yet:

5 "But what proof have you, Mr. Harris?"

"I told you. The hog got into my corn. I caught it up and sent it back to him. He had no fence that would hold it. I told him so, warned him. The next time I put the hog in my pen. When he came to get it I gave him
10 enough wire to patch up his pen. The next time I put the hog up and kept it. I rode down to his house and saw the wire I gave him still rolled on to the spool in his yard. I told him he could have the hog when he paid me a dollar pound fee. That evening a nigger came with
15 the dollar and got the hog. He was a strange nigger. He said, 'He say to tell you wood and hay kin burn.' I said, 'What?' 'That whut he say to tell you,' the nigger said. 'Wood and hay kin burn.' That night my barn burned. I got the stock out but I lost the barn."

20 "Where is the nigger? Have you got him?"

"He was a strange nigger, I tell you. I don't know what became of him."

"But that's not proof. Don't you see that's not proof?"

25 "Get that boy up here. He knows." For a moment the boy thought too that the man meant his older brother until Harris said, "Not him. The little one. The boy,"

---

2 **ourn! mine and hisn** (dial.): *ours! mine and his.*
12 **spool:** Spule.
14 **dollar pound fee:** hier: Stallgebühr in Höhe von einem Dollar.
16 **kin** (dial.): *can.*
17 **whut** (dial.): *what.*
19 **stock:** Vieh.

and, crouching, small for his age, small and wiry like his
father, in patched and faded jeans even too small for
him, with straight, uncombed, brown hair and eyes gray
and wild as storm scud, he saw the men between himself and the table part and become a lane of grim faces,
at the end of which he saw the Justice, a shabby, collarless, graying man in spectacles, beckoning him. He felt
no floor under his bare feet; he seemed to walk beneath the palpable weight of the grim turning faces. His
father, stiff in his black Sunday coat donned not for the
trial but for the moving, did not even look at him. *He
aims for me to lie*, he thought, again with that frantic
grief and despair. *And I will have to do hit.*

"What's your name, boy?" the Justice said.

"Colonel Sartoris Snopes," the boy whispered.

"Hey?" the Justice said. "Talk louder. Colonel Sartoris? I reckon anybody named for Colonel Sartoris in
this country can't help but tell the truth, can they?" The
boy said nothing. *Enemy! Enemy!* he thought; for a
moment he could not even see, could not see that the
Justice's face was kindly nor discern that his voice was

---

1 **wiry:** drahtig.
4 **storm scud:** Regen-, Gewitterwolken.
5 **to part:** hier: auseinanderweichen.
6 **shabby:** ärmlich gekleidet.
7 **to beckon:** heranwinken.
9 **palpable:** spürbar.
10 **to don:** (Kleidung) anlegen.
11 **moving:** hier: Umzug.
11 f. **he aims for me to lie:** er will, daß ich lüge.
12 **frantic:** wild.
13 **hit** (dial.): *it.*
21 **kindly:** freundlich.
   to discern: merken, bemerken.

troubled when he spoke to the man named Harris: "Do
you want me to question this boy?" But he could hear,
and during those subsequent long seconds while there
was absolutely no sound in the crowded little room
5 save that of quiet and intent breathing it was as if he
had swung outward at the end of a grape vine, over a
ravine, and at the top of the swing had been caught in
a prolonged instant of mesmerized gravity, weightless
in time.

10 "No!" Harris said violently, explosively. "Damnation!
Send him out of here!" Now time, the fluid world,
rushed beneath him again, the voices coming to him
again through the smell of cheese and sealed meat, the
fear and despair and the old grief of blood:

15 "This case is closed. I can't find against you, Snopes,
but I can give you advice. Leave this country and don't
come back to it."
His father spoke for the first time, his voice cold and
harsh, level, without emphasis: "I aim to. I don't figure
20 to stay in a country among people who ..." he said
something unprintable and vile, addressed to no one.

---

3 **subsequent:** folgend.
5 **intent:** konzentriert, gespannt.
6 **grape vine:** Weinstock, -ranke.
7 **ravine:** Abgrund, Schlucht.
8 **mesmerized:** erstarrt, gebannt.
  gravity: Schwerkraft.
10 **damnation:** verdammt!, zum Teufel!
13 **sealed meat:** Fleischkonserven.
15 **this case is closed:** der Fall ist abgeschlossen.
19 **harsh:** rauh.
  to aim to: im Sinn haben, beabsichtigen.
  to figure: denken; hier auch: die Absicht haben.
21 **unprintable and vile:** anstößig und schmutzig.

"That'll do," the Justice said. "Take your wagon and get out of this country before dark. Case dismissed."

His father turned, and he followed the stiff black coat, the wiry figure walking a little stiffly from where a Confederate provost's man's musket ball had taken him in the heel on a stolen horse thirty years ago,[2] followed the two backs now, since his older brother had appeared from somewhere in the crowd, no taller than the father but thicker, chewing tobacco steadily, between the two lines of grim-faced men and out of the store and across the worn gallery and down the sagging steps and among the dogs and half-grown boys in the mild May dust, where as he passed a voice hissed: "Barn burner!"

Again he could not see, whirling; there was a face in a red haze, moonlike, bigger than the full moon, the owner of it half again his size, he leaping in the red haze toward the face, feeling no blow, feeling no shock when his head struck the earth, scrabbling up and leaping again, feeling no blow this time either and tasting no blood, scrabbling up to see the other boy in full flight and himself already leaping into pursuit as his fa-

---

1 **that'll do!:** genug!
2 **case dismissed:** der Fall ist erledigt.
4 f. **Confederate:** konföderiert, Südstaaten- (vgl. Anm. 2).
5 **provost:** Offizier der Militärpolizei.
   musket: Muskete (alte Handfeuerwaffe).
11 **worn:** abgenutzt.
   gallery: hier: Veranda.
   sagging: ab-, durchgesackt.
13 **to hiss:** (nach)zischen.
15 **to whirl:** herumwirbeln, sich schnell herumdrehen.
16 **haze:** Dunstschleier.
19 **to scrabble up:** sich hochrappeln, Halt suchen.

ther's hand jerked him back, the harsh, cold voice
speaking above him: "Go get in the wagon."
It stood in a grove of locusts and mulberries across the
road. His two hulking sisters in their Sunday dresses
5 and his mother and her sister in calico and sunbonnets
were already in it, sitting on and among the sorry residue of the dozen and more movings which even the boy
could remember – the battered stove, the broken beds
and chairs, the clock inlaid with mother-of-pearl, which
10 would not run, stopped at some fourteen minutes past
two o'clock of a dead and forgotten day and time,
which had been his mother's dowry. She was crying,
though when she saw him she drew her sleeve across
her face and began to descend from the wagon.
15 "Get back," the father said.
"He's hurt. I got to get some water and wash his . . ."
"Get back in the wagon," his father said. He got in too,
over the tail-gate. His father mounted to the seat where
the older brother already sat and struck the gaunt
20 mules two savage blows with the peeled willow, but

---

1 **to jerk back:** zurückreißen.
3 **grove:** Gehölz, Wäldchen.
　locust: Robinie.
　mulberry: Maulbeerbaum.
4 **hulking:** unförmig.
5 **calico:** Kattun.
　sunbonnet: Sonnenhut, -haube.
6 f. **residue:** Überbleibsel.
8 **battered:** zerbeult.
9 **inlaid with mother-of-pearl:** mit Perlmutt eingelegt.
12 **dowry:** Mitgift.
18 **tail-gate:** rückwärtige Wagenklappe, Heckklappe.
19 **gaunt:** hager.
20 **mule:** Maultier.
　willow: Weidengerte.

without heat. It was not even sadistic; it was exactly that same quality which in later years would cause his descendants to over-run the engine before putting a motor car into motion, striking and reining back in the same movement. The wagon went on, the store with its quiet crowd of grimly watching men dropped behind; a curve in the road hid it. *Forever* he thought. *Maybe he's done satisfied now, now that he has ...* stopping himself, not to say it aloud even to himself. His mother's hand touched his shoulder.

"Does hit hurt?" she said.

"Naw," he said. "Hit don't hurt. Lemme be."

"Can't you wipe some of the blood off before hit dries?"

"I'll wash to-night," he said. "Lemme be, I tell you."

The wagon went on. He did not know where they were going. None of them ever did or ever asked, because it was always somewhere, always a house of sorts waiting for them a day or two days or even three days away. Likely his father had already arranged to make a crop on another farm before he ... Again he had to stop himself. He (the father) always did. There was something about his wolflike independence and even courage when the advantage was at least neutral which impressed strangers, as if they got from his latent raven-

---

4 **to rein back:** zügeln.

7 f. **Maybe he's done satisfied now:** Vielleicht ist er jetzt endlich zufrieden.

12 **naw** (dial.): *no*.

   lemme be (dial.): *let me be:* laß mich in Ruh.

18 **a house of sorts:** irgendein Haus.

25 **latent:** verborgen.

25 f. **ravening:** wild, gierig.

ing ferocity not so much a sense of dependability as a feeling that his ferocious conviction in the rightness of his own actions would be of advantage to all whose interest lay with his.

5 That night they camped, in a grove of oaks and beeches where a spring ran. The nights were still cool and they had a fire against it, of a rail lifted from a nearby fence and cut into lengths – a small fire, neat, niggard almost, a shrewd fire; such fires were his father's habit and cus-
10 tom always, even in freezing weather. Older, the boy might have remarked this and wondered why not a big one; why should not a man who had not only seen the waste and extravagance of war, but who had in his blood an inherent voracious prodigality with material
15 not his own, have burned everything in sight? Then he might have gone a step farther and thought that that was the reason: that niggard blaze was the living fruit of nights passed during those four years in the woods hiding from all men, blue or gray,[3] with his strings of
20 horses (captured horses, he called them). And older still, he might have divined the true reason: that the element of fire spoke to some deep mainspring of his

---

1 **ferocity:** Wildheit.
   dependability: Zuverlässigkeit.
2 **ferocious:** grimmig, heftig.
5 **beech:** Buche.
8 **niggard:** knauserig, karg.
9 **shrewd:** klug, gerissen.
10 **freezing:** Frost-.
14 **voracious:** unersättlich.
   prodigality: Verschwendungssucht.
17 **blaze:** Feuer.
21 **to divine:** ahnen, erraten.
22 **mainspring:** Haupttriebfeder.

father's being, as the element of steel or of powder spoke to other men, as the one weapon for the preservation of integrity, else breath were not worth the breathing, and hence to be regarded with respect and
5 used with discretion.
But he did not think this now and he had seen those same niggard blazes all his life. He merely ate his supper beside it and was already half asleep over his iron plate when his father called him, and once more he fol-
10 lowed the stiff back, the stiff and ruthless limp, up the slope and on to the starlit road where, turning, he could see his father against the stars but without face or depth – a shape black, flat, and bloodless as though cut from tin in the iron folds of the frockcoat which had
15 not been made for him, the voice harsh like tin and without heat like tin:
"You were fixing to tell them. You would have told him." He didn't answer. His father struck him with the flat of his hand on the side of the head, hard but with-
20 out heat, exactly as he had struck the two mules at the store, exactly as he would strike either of them with any stick in order to kill a horse fly, his voice still without heat or anger: "You're getting to be a man. You got to learn. You got to learn to stick to your own blood or

3 **integrity:** Integrität, Ganzheit; Echtheit.
5 **discretion:** Besonnenheit.
10 **ruthless:** rücksichtslos.
   limp: Hinken.
11 **starlit:** sternhell.
14 **frockcoat:** Gehrock.
17 **You were fixing to tell them:** Du wolltest es ihnen sagen.
19 **flat of the hand:** Handfläche.
22 **horse fly:** Pferdebremse.

you ain't going to have any blood to stick to you. Do
you think either of them, any man there this morning,
would? Don't you know all they wanted was a chance
to get at me because they knew I had them beat? Eh?"
5 Later, twenty years later, he was to tell himself, "If I
had said they wanted only truth, justice, he would have
hit me again." But now he said nothing. He was not
crying. He just stood there. "Answer me," his father
said.
10 "Yes," he whispered. His father turned.
"Get on to bed. We'll be there to-morrow."
To-morrow they were there. In the early afternoon the
wagon stopped before a paintless two-room house
identical almost with the dozen others it had stopped
15 before even in the boy's ten years, and again, as on the
other dozen occasions, his mother and aunt got down
and began to unload the wagon, although his two sisters and his father and brother had not moved.
"Likely hit ain't fitten for hawgs," one of the sisters
20 said.
"Nevertheless, fit it will and you'll hog it and like it,"
his father said. "Get out of them chairs and help your
Ma unload."
The two sisters got down, big, bovine, in a flutter of

1 **ain't** (dial.): *are not.*
4 **to get at s.o.:** jdn. unter Druck setzen; über jdn. herfallen.
   I had them beat (dial.): *I had beaten them.*
19 **hit ain't fitten for** (dial.): *it is not fit for.*
   hawg (dial.): *hog.*
21 **to hog s.th.:** etwas mit Beschlag belegen; hier: sich an etwas gewöh-
   nen.
22 **them** (dial.): *those.*
24 **bovine** (fig.): grob, schwerfällig.
   in a flutter: umflattert.

cheap ribbons; one of them drew from the jumbled wagon bed a battered lantern, the other a worn broom. His father handed the reins to the older son and began to climb stiffly over the wheel. "When they get unload-
5 ed, take the team to the barn and feed them." Then he said, and at first the boy thought he was still speaking to his brother: "Come with me."

"Me?" he said.

"Yes," his father said. "You."

10 "Abner," his mother said. His father paused and looked back – the harsh level stare beneath the shaggy, graying, irascible brows.

"I reckon I'll have a word with the man that aims to be-gin to-morrow owning me body and soul for the next
15 eight months."[4]

They went back up the road. A week ago – or before last night, that is – he would have asked where they were going, but not now. His father had struck him before last night but never before had he paused after-
20 ward to explain why; it was as if the blow and the fol-lowing calm, outrageous voice still rang, repercussed, divulging nothing to him save the terrible handicap of being young, the light weight of his few years, just

---

1 **to jumble:** in Unordnung bringen.
2 **wagon bed:** Wagenkasten.
  lantern: Laterne.
3 **reins** (pl.): Zügel.
11 **shaggy:** struppig.
12 **irascible:** reizbar.
  brow: Braue.
21 **outrageous:** unerhört, ungeheuerlich.
  to repercuss: widerhallen.
22 **to divulge:** verraten.

heavy enough to prevent his soaring free of the world as it seemed to be ordered but not heavy enough to keep him footed solid in it, to resist it and try to change the course of its events.

5 Presently he could see the grove of oaks and cedars and the other flowering trees and shrubs where the house would be, though not the house yet. They walked beside a fence massed with honeysuckle and Cherokee roses and came to a gate swinging open between two
10 brick pillars, and now, beyond a sweep of drive, he saw the house for the first time and at that instant he forgot his father and the terror and despair both, and even when he remembered his father again (who had not stopped) the terror and despair did not return. Be-
15 cause, for all the twelve movings, they had sojourned until now in a poor country, a land of small farms and fields and houses, and he had never seen a house like this before. *Hit's big as a courthouse* he thought quietly, with a surge of peace and joy whose reason he could
20 not have thought into words, being too young for that: *They are safe from him. People whose lives are a part of this peace and dignity are beyond his touch, he no more*

---

1 **to soar:** davonfliegen.
3 **to keep s.o. footed solid in the world:** jdn. fest auf der Erde halten.
5 **cedar:** Zeder.
6 **shrub:** Busch.
8 (*to be*) **massed with s.th.:** hier: von etwas überwuchert sein.
  honeysuckle: Geißblatt.
8 f. **Cherokee rose:** weiße Rosenart.
10 **sweep of drive:** bogenförmige Auffahrt.
15 **to sojourn:** sich aufhalten.
18 **courthouse:** Gerichts-, Amtsgebäude.
19 **surge:** Aufwallung.
22 **to be beyond s.o.'s touch:** für jdn. unerreichbar sein.

to them than a buzzing wasp: capable of stinging for a
little moment but that's all; the spell of this peace and
dignity rendering even the barns and stable and cribs
which belong to it impervious to the puny flames he
5 *might contrive . . .* this, the peace and joy, ebbing for an
instant as he looked again at the stiff black back, the
stiff and implacable limp of the figure which was not
dwarfed by the house, for the reason that it had never
looked big anywhere and which now, against the serene
10 columned backdrop, had more than ever that impervious quality of something cut ruthlessly from tin, depthless, as though, sidewise to the sun, it would cast no
shadow. Watching him, the boy remarked the absolutely undeviating course which his father held and saw
15 the stiff foot come squarely down in a pile of fresh
droppings where a horse had stood in the drive and
which his father could have avoided by a simple change
of stride. But it ebbed only for a moment, though he
could not have thought this into words either, walking

1 **to buzz:** summen, sirren.
2 **spell:** Zauber, Bann.
3 **crib:** (Futter-)Krippe.
4 **impervious:** unangreifbar, undurchdringlich.
   puny: schwächlich.
5 **to contrive:** zustande bringen.
   to ebb: verebben, abnehmen.
7 **implacable:** unerbittlich.
8 **to dwarf:** klein erscheinen lassen.
9 **serene:** heiter.
10 **backdrop:** Hintergrund.
12 **sidewise:** seitwärts.
14 **undeviating:** unbeirrbar.
15 **to come squarely down in s.th.:** mitten in etwas hinein treten.
16 **droppings** (pl.): Dung, Mist.
17 f. **change of stride:** Schrittwechsel.

on in the spell of the house, which he could even want
but without envy, without sorrow, certainly never with
that ravening and jealous rage which unknown to him
walked in the ironlike black coat before him: *Maybe he*
will feel it too. Maybe it will even change him now from
what maybe he couldn't help but be.

They crossed the portico. Now he could hear his father's stiff foot as it came down on the boards with
clocklike finality, a sound out of all proportion to the
displacement of the body it bore and which was not
dwarfed either by the white door before it, as though it
had attained to a sort of vicious and ravening minimum
not to be dwarfed by anything – the flat, wide, black
hat, the formal coat of broadcloth which had once
been black but which had now that friction-glazed
greenish cast of the bodies of old house flies, the lifted
sleeve which was too large, the lifted hand like a curled
claw. The door opened so promptly that the boy knew
the Negro must have been watching them all the time,
an old man with neat grizzled hair, in a linen jacket,
who stood barring the door with his body, saying,

---

2 **sorrow:** hier: Bedauern.
7 **portico:** Säulenvorbau.
9 **finality:** Endgültigkeit, Entschiedenheit, Bestimmtheit.
10 **displacement:** Verdrängung (von Gewicht).
12 **to attain:** erreichen.
14 **broadcloth:** besondere, schwere Stoffart.
15 **friction-glazed:** durch häufiges Reiben blank geworden.
16 **cast:** Schimmer.
17 **curled:** hier: gekrümmt.
18 **claw:** Klaue.
20 **grizzled:** grau, ergraut.
   linen jacket: Leinenjacke.
21 **to bar:** versperren.

16

"Wipe yo foots, white man, fo you come in here. Major ain't home nohow."

"Get out of my way, nigger," his father said, without heat too, flinging the door back and the Negro also and
5 entering, his hat still on his head. And now the boy saw the prints of the stiff foot on the doorjamb and saw them appear on the pale rug behind the machinelike deliberation of the foot which seemed to bear (or transmit) twice the weight which the body compassed. The
10 Negro was shouting "Miss Lula! Miss Lula!" somewhere behind them, then the boy, deluged as though by a warm wave by a suave turn of carpeted stair and a pendant glitter of chandeliers and a mute gleam of gold frames, heard the swift feet and saw her too, a lady –
15 perhaps he had never seen her like before either – in a gray, smooth gown with lace at the throat and an apron

---

1 **yo** (dial.): *your*.
  foots (dial.): *feet*.
  fo (dial.): *before*.
2 **nohow** (dial.): *anyway*.
4 **to fling back:** zurückwerfen.
6 **doorjamb:** Türschwelle.
8 **deliberation:** Absicht, Entschlossenheit.
8 f. **to transmit:** übermitteln.
9 **to compass:** umfassen.
11 **to deluge:** überfluten.
12 **suave:** schön geschwungen, elegant.
13 **pendant:** herabhängend.
  glitter: Glitzern.
  chandelier: Kristalleuchter.
  mute: still, stumm.
  gleam: Glanz.
16 **smooth:** weich, fließend.
  gown: Kleid, Gewand.
  lace: (Stoff-)Spitze(n).
  apron: Schürze.

tied at the waist and the sleeves turned back, wiping
cake or biscuit dough from her hands with a towel as
she came up the hall, looking not at his father at all but
at the tracks on the blond rug with an expression of in-
5 credulous amazement.

"I tried," the Negro cried. "I tole him to ..."

"Will you please go away?" she said in a shaking voice.
"Major de Spain is not at home. Will you please go
away?"

10 His father had not spoken again. He did not speak
again. He did not even look at her. He just stood stiff
in the center of the rug, in his hat, the shaggy iron-gray
brows twitching slightly above the pebble-colored eyes
as he appeared to examine the house with brief delibe-
15 ration. Then with the same deliberation he turned; the
boy watched him pivot on the good leg and saw the stiff
foot drag round the arc of the turning, leaving a final
long and fading smear. His father never looked at it, he
never once looked down at the rug. The Negro held the
20 door. It closed behind them, upon the hysteric and indistinguishable woman-wail. His father stopped at the
top of the steps and scraped his boot clean on the edge
of it. At the gate he stopped again. He stood for a moment, planted stiffly on the stiff foot, looking back at

---

2 **dough:** Teig.
4 f. **incredulous:** ungläubig.
6 **tole** (dial.): *told.*
13 **to twitch:** zucken.
   pebble-colored: kieselgrau.
16 **to pivot:** sich drehen.
17 **arc:** (Kreis-)Bogen.
20 f. **indistinguishable:** nicht unterscheidbar.
21 **woman-wail:** Frauenklagen, -jammern.

18

the house. "Pretty and white, ain't it?" he said. "That's sweat. Nigger sweat. Maybe it ain't white enough yet to suit him. Maybe he wants to mix some white sweat with it."

5 Two hours later the boy was chopping wood behind the house within which his mother and aunt and the two sisters (the mother and aunt, not the two girls, he knew that; even at this distance and muffled by walls the flat loud voices of the two girls emanated an incorrigible
10 idle inertia) were setting up the stove to prepare a meal, when he heard the hooves and saw the linen-clad man on a fine sorrel mare, whom he recognized even before he saw the rolled rug in front of the Negro youth following on a fat bay carriage horse – a suf-
15 fused, angry face vanishing, still at full gallop, beyond the corner of the house where his father and brother were sitting in the two tilted chairs; and a moment later, almost before he could have put the axe down, he heard the hooves again and watched the sorrel mare go
20 back out of the yard, already galloping again. Then his father began to shout one of the sisters' names, who presently emerged backward from the kitchen door

---

8 **muffled:** gedämpft (Geräusch).
9 **to emanate:** (fig.) ausstrahlen.
   incorrigible: nicht zu korrigieren, unausrottbar.
10 **inertia:** Trägheit.
11 **linen-clad:** in Leinen gekleidet.
12 **sorrel:** fuchsrot, rotbraun.
   mare: Stute.
14 **bay:** braun (Pferd).
   carriage: Wagen, Kutsche.
14 f. **to suffuse:** übergießen, -ziehen, tauchen, tränken.
17 **to tilt:** kippen, schräg stellen.

dragging the rolled rug along the ground by one end
while the other sister walked behind it.

"If you ain't going to tote, go on and set up the wash
pot," the first said.

5 "You, Sarty!" the second shouted. "Set up the wash
pot!" His father appeared at the door, framed against
that shabbiness, as he had been against that other
bland perfection, impervious to either, the mother's
anxious face at his shoulder.

10 "Go on," the father said. "Pick it up." The two sisters
stooped, broad, lethargic; stooping, they presented an
incredible expanse of pale cloth and a flutter of tawdry
ribbons.

"If I thought enough of a rug to have to git hit all the
15 way from France I wouldn't keep hit where folks coming in would have to tromp on hit," the first said. They
raised the rug.

"Abner," the mother said. "Let me do it."

"You go back and git dinner," his father said. "I'll tend
20 to this."

From the woodpile through the rest of the afternoon
the boy watched them, the rug spread flat in the dust
beside the bubbling wash-pot, the two sisters stooping
over it with that profound and lethargic reluctance,

---

3 **to tote** (dial.): tragen.
7 **shabbiness:** Schäbigkeit, Ärmlichkeit.
8 **bland:** unverbindlich, neutral.
11 **to stoop:** sich bücken.
12 **expanse:** Ausdehnung, Fülle.
   tawdry: billig, grell.
14 **git** (dial.): *get*.
15 **folks:** Leute.
16 **to tromp** (dial.): treten.
21 **woodpile:** Holzhaufen.

Inhalt

Fremdsprachentexte

IN RECLAMS UNIVERSAL-BIBLIOTHEK

Englische und amerikanische Dramen

Auswahl

Philipp Reclam jun. Stuttgart

while the father stood over them in turn, implacable and grim, driving them though never raising his voice again. He could smell the harsh homemade lye they were using; he saw his mother come to the door once and look toward them with an expression not anxious now but very like despair; he saw his father turn, and he fell to with the axe and saw from the corner of his eye his father raise from the ground a flattish fragment of field stone and examine it and return to the pot, and this time his mother actually spoke: "Abner. Abner. Please don't. Please, Abner."

Then he was done too. It was dusk; the whippoorwills had already begun. He could smell coffee from the room where they would presently eat the cold food remaining from the mid-afternoon meal, though when he entered the house he realized they were having coffee again probably because there was a fire on the hearth, before which the rug now lay spread over the backs of the two chairs. The tracks of his father's foot were gone. Where they had been were now long, water-cloudy scoriations resembling the sporadic course of a lilliputian mowing machine.

It still hung there while they ate the cold food and then

---

3 **lye:** Lauge.
7 **to fall to:** sich dranmachen.
8 **flattish:** flach.
 fragment: Stückchen.
12 **dusk:** (Abend-)Dämmerung.
 whippoorwill: Ziegenmelker, Nachtschwalbe.
17 **hearth:** Herd.
21 **scoriations:** Markierungen, Spuren.
 sporadic: hier: zufällig.
22 **mowing machine:** Mähmaschine, Mäher.

went to bed, scattered without order or claim up and
down the two rooms, his mother in one bed, where his
father would later lie, the older brother in the other,
himself, the aunt, and the two sisters on pallets on the
5 floor. But his father was not in bed yet. The last thing
the boy remembered was the depthless, harsh silhouette of the hat and coat bending over the rug and it
seemed to him that he had not even closed his eyes
when the silhouette was standing over him, the fire al-
10 most dead behind it, the stiff foot prodding him awake.
"Catch up the mule," his father said.
When he returned with the mule his father was standing in the black door, the rolled rug over his shoulder.
"Ain't you going to ride?" he said.
15 "No. Give me your foot."
He bent his knee into his father's hand, the wiry, sur-
prising power flowed smoothly, rising, he rising with it,
on to the mule's bare back (they had owned a saddle
once; the boy could remember it though not when or
20 where) and with the same effortlessness his father
swung the rug up in front of him. Now in the starlight
they retraced the afternoon's path, up the dusty road
rife with honeysuckle, through the gate and up the
black tunnel of the drive to the lightless house, where
25 he sat on the mule and felt the rough warp of the rug
drag across his thighs and vanish.

---

1 **scattered:** verteilt.
4 **pallet:** Pritsche, einfaches Bett.
10 **to prod:** stoßen.
20 **effortlessness:** Mühelosigkeit.
22 **to retrace:** zurückverfolgen.
23 (to be) **rife with s.th.:** voll von etwas sein.
25 **warp:** Gewebe.
26 **thigh:** (Ober-)Schenkel.

22

"Don't you want me to help?" he whispered. His father did not answer and now he heard again that stiff foot striking the hollow portico with that wooden and clock-like deliberation, that outrageous overstatement of the
5 weight it carried. The rug, hunched, not flung (the boy could tell that even in the darkness) from his father's shoulder struck the angle of wall and floor with a sound unbelievably loud, thunderous, then the foot again, un-hurried and enormous; a light came on in the house
10 and the boy sat, tense, breathing steadily and quietly and just a little fast, though the foot itself did not in-crease its beat at all, descending the steps now; now the boy could see him.

"Don't you want to ride now?" he whispered. "We kin
15 both ride now," the light within the house altering now, flaring up and sinking. *He's coming down the stairs now*, he thought. He had already ridden the mule up beside the horse block; presently his father was up behind him and he doubled the reins over and slashed the mule
20 across the neck, but before the animal could begin to trot the hard, thin arm came round him, the hard, knot-ted hand jerking the mule back to a walk.

---

4 **overstatement:** Übertreibung.
5 **to hunch:** (sich) zusammenrollen; hier: gerollt fallen lassen.
8 **thunderous:** donnernd.
12 **beat:** Takt, Rhythmus.
16 **to flare up:** aufflackern.
18 **horse block:** Block zum Aufsitzen.
19 **to double the reins over:** die (beiden) Zügel miteinander verbin-den.
   to slash: schlagen.
21 **to trot:** traben.
21 f. **knotted:** knotig.
22 **walk:** Schritt (Pferdegangart).

In the first red rays of the sun they were in the lot, putting plow gear on the mules. This time the sorrel mare was in the lot before he heard it at all, the rider collarless and even bareheaded, trembling, speaking in a shaking voice as the woman in the house had done, his father merely looking up once before stooping again to the hame he was buckling, so that the man on the mare spoke to his stooping back:

"You must realize you have ruined that rug. Wasn't there anybody here, any of your women . . ." he ceased, shaking, the boy watching him, the older brother leaning now in the stable door, chewing, blinking slowly and steadily at nothing apparently. "It cost a hundred dollars. But you never had a hundred dollars. You never will. So I'm going to charge you twenty bushels of corn against your crop. I'll add it in your contract and when you come to the commissary you can sign it.[5] That won't keep Mrs. de Spain quiet but maybe it will teach you to wipe your feet off before you enter her house again."

Then he was gone. The boy looked at his father, who still had not spoken or even looked up again, who was now adjusting the logger-head in the hame.

---

1 **lot:** hier: Hofplatz.
2 **plow gear:** Pfluggeschirr.
4 **bareheaded:** barhäuptig.
7 **hame:** Kummet (Teil des [Pferde-]Geschirrs; gepolsterter Leder- oder Stoffbalg).
  to buckle: festschnallen.
12 **to blink:** blinzeln.
15 **to charge:** in Rechnung stellen.
  bushel: Scheffel (Getreidemaß).
17 **commissary:** Laden (vgl. Anm. 5).
23 **logger-head:** Zughaken (zur Befestigung der Steuerketten und Zugstränge am Kummet).

"Pap," he said. His father looked at him – the inscrutable face, the shaggy brows beneath which the gray eyes glinted coldly. Suddenly the boy went toward him, fast, stopping as suddenly. "You done the best you could!" he cried. "If he wanted hit done different why didn't he wait and tell you how? He won't git no twenty bushels! He won't git none! We'll gether hit and hide hit! I kin watch . . ."

"Did you put the cutter back in that straight stock like I told you?"

"No, sir," he said.

"Then go do it."

That was Wednesday. During the rest of that week he worked steadily, at what was within his scope and some which was beyond it, with an industry that did not need to be driven nor even commanded twice; he had this from his mother, with the difference that some at least of what he did he liked to do, such as splitting wood with the half-size axe which his mother and aunt had earned, or saved money somehow, to present him with at Christmas. In company with the two older women (and on one afternoon, even one of the sisters), he built pens for the shoat and the cow which were a part of his father's contract with the landlord, and one afternoon,

---

1 f. **inscrutable:** undurchdringlich.
3 **to glint:** funkeln, glitzern.
7 **gether** (dial.): *gather.*
9 **cutter:** Kolter, Pflugmesser.
   straight stock: Rahmen eines einfachen Pfluges.
14 **scope:** Aufgabenbereich.
15 **industry:** Fleiß, Eifer.
23 **shoat:** Ferkel.
24 **landlord:** Vermieter; hier: Pachtherr.

his father being absent, gone somewhere on one of the
mules, he went to the field.

They were running a middle buster now, his brother
holding the plow straight while he handled the reins,
5 and walking beside the straining mule, the rich black
soil shearing cool and damp against his bare ankles, he
thought *Maybe this is the end of it. Maybe even that
twenty bushels that seems hard to have to pay for just a
rug will be a cheap price for him to stop forever and al-
10 ways from being what he used to be*; thinking, dreaming
now, so that his brother had to speak sharply to him
to mind the mule: *Maybe he even won't collect the twenty bushels. Maybe it will all add up and balance and vanish – corn, rug, fire; the terror and grief, the being
15 pulled two ways like between two teams of horses –
gone, done with for ever and ever.*

Then it was Saturday; he looked up from beneath the
mule he was harnessing and saw his father in the black
coat and hat. "Not that," his father said. "The wagon
20 gear." And then, two hours later, sitting in the wagon
bed behind his father and brother on the seat, the
wagon accomplished a final curve, and he saw the

---

3 **to run:** bedienen, einsetzen.
   middle buster: Pflug zum Häufeln von Pflanzen.
6 **to shear:** hier etwa: sich wölben, entgegenkommen.
10 **what he used to be:** was er bisher war.
12 **to collect:** abholen.
13 **to add up:** sich summieren.
14 f. **the being pulled two ways:** das Hinundhergerissensein.
16 **done with:** erledigt.
18 **to harness:** anschirren.
19 f. **wagon gear:** Wagengeschirr.
22 **to accomplish:** vollenden.

weathered paintless store with its tattered tobacco- and patent-medicine posters and the tethered wagons and saddle animals below the gallery. He mounted the gnawed steps behind his father and brother, and there again was the lane of quiet, watching faces for the three of them to walk through. He saw the man in spectacles sitting at the plank table and he did not need to be told this was a Justice of the Peace; he sent one glare of fierce, exultant, partisan defiance at the man in collar and cravat now, whom he had seen but twice before in his life, and that on a galloping horse, who now wore on his face an expression not of rage but of amazed unbelief which the boy could not have known was at the incredible circumstance of being sued by one of his own tenants, and came and stood against his father and cried at the Justice: "He ain't done it! He ain't burnt . . ."

"Go back to the wagon," his father said.

"Burnt?" the Justice said. "Do I understand this rug was burned too?"

"Does anybody here claim it was?" his father said. "Go back to the wagon." But he did not, he merely retreat-

---

1 **tattered:** zerfetzt, zerfleddert.
2 **to tether:** anpflocken, -binden.
3 **to mount:** hinaufsteigen.
4 **gnawed:** wörtl.: abgenagt; hier: ausgetreten.
7 **plank:** Brett.
8 **glare:** scharfer Blick.
9 **exultant:** triumphierend.
  partisan: parteiisch.
  defiance: Herausforderung, Trotz.
10 **cravat:** Krawatte.
15 **tenant:** Pächter.
16 **ain't** (dial.): *has not.*

ed to the rear of the room, crowded as that other had
been, but not to sit down this time, instead, to stand
pressing among the motionless bodies, listening to the
voices:

5 "And you claim twenty bushels of corn is too high for
the damage you did to the rug?"
"He brought the rug to me and said he wanted the
tracks washed out of it. I washed the tracks out and
took the rug back to him."

10 "But you didn't carry the rug back to him in the same
condition it was in before you made the tracks on it."
His father did not answer, and now for perhaps half a
minute there was no sound at all save that of breathing,
the faint, steady suspiration of complete and intent lis-

15 tening.
"You decline to answer that, Mr. Snopes?" Again his
father did not answer. "I'm going to find against you,
Mr. Snopes. I'm going to find that you were responsible
for the injury to Major de Spain's rug and hold you lia-

20 ble for it. But twenty bushels of corn seems a little high
for a man in your circumstances to have to pay. Major
de Spain claims it cost a hundred dollars. October corn
will be worth about fifty cents. I figure that if Major de
Spain can stand a ninety-five dollar loss on something

25 he paid cash for, you can stand a five-dollar loss you
haven't earned yet. I hold you in damages to Major de

---

1 **rear:** hinterer Teil.
3 **to press:** (sich) drücken, drängen.
14 **suspiration:** Atemholen.
19 **injury:** hier: Schaden.
19 f. **to hold s.o. liable for s.th.:** jdn. für etwas haftbar machen.
24 **to stand s.th.:** etwas ertragen, verkraften.
26 **to hold s.o. in damages:** jdn. zu Schadensersatz verurteilen.

Spain to the amount of ten bushels of corn over and above your contract with him, to be paid to him out of your crop at gathering time. Court adjourned."

It had taken no time hardly, the morning was but half begun. He thought they would return home and perhaps back to the field, since they were late, far behind all other farmers. But instead his father passed on behind the wagon, merely indicating with his hand for the older brother to follow with it, and crossed the road toward the blacksmith shop opposite, pressing on after his father, overtaking him, speaking, whispering up at the harsh, calm face beneath the weathered hat: "He won't git no ten bushels neither. He won't git one. We'll . . ." until his father glanced for an instant down at him, the face absolutely calm, the grizzled eyebrows tangled above the cold eyes, the voice almost pleasant, almost gentle:

"You think so? Well, we'll wait till October anyway."

The matter of the wagon – the setting of a spoke or two and the tightening of the tires – did not take long either, the business of the tires accomplished by driving the wagon into the spring branch behind the shop and letting it stand there, the mules nuzzling into the water from time to time, and the boy on the seat with the idle

---

3 **gathering time:** Ernte.
   court adjourned: die Sitzung ist geschlossen.
7 **to pass on:** hier: weitergehen.
10 **blacksmith shop:** Schmiede.
16 **tangled:** verfilzt, struppig.
19 **spoke:** Speiche.
20 **to tighten:** festziehen.
22 **spring branch:** Bach, Quellwasser.
23 **to nuzzle into s.th.:** das Maul in etwas drücken, vorstrecken.

reins, looking up the slope and through the sooty tunnel of the shed where the slow hammer rang and where his father sat on an upended cypress bolt, easily, either talking or listening, still sitting there when the boy
5 brought the dripping wagon up out of the branch and halted it before the door.

"Take them on to the shade and hitch," his father said. He did so and returned. His father and the smith and a third man squatting on his heels inside the door were
10 talking, about crops and animals; the boy, squatting too in the ammoniac dust and hoof-parings and scales of rust, heard his father tell a long and unhurried story out of the time before the birth of the older brother even when he had been a professional horsetrader. And then
15 his father came up beside him where he stood before a tattered last year's circus poster on the other side of the store, gazing rapt and quiet at the scarlet horses, the incredible poisings and convolutions of tulle and

---

1 **sooty:** verrußt.
2 **to ring:** (er)dröhnen.
3 **upended:** umgedreht.
   cypress bolt: Stumpf einer Zypresse.
6 **to halt:** anhalten.
7 **to hitch:** (Pferd) festbinden.
8 **smith:** Schmied.
10 **to squat:** hocken.
11 **ammoniac:** ammoniakalisch, ammoniakhaltig; nach Harn stinkend.
   hoof-parings: von den Hufen abgefeilte Späne.
11 f. **scales of rust:** Rostflocken.
14 **horsetrader:** Pferdehändler.
17 **to gaze at s.th.:** etwas betrachten, anstarren.
   rapt: hingerissen.
   scarlet: purpurrot.
18 **poising:** (Körper-)Haltung.
   convolution: Windung, Verrenkung.
   tulle: Tüll.

tights and the painted leers of comedians, and said, "It's time to eat."

But not at home. Squatting beside his brother against the front wall, he watched his father emerge from the store and produce from a paper sack a segment of cheese and divide it carefully and deliberately into three with his pocket knife and produce crackers from the same sack. They all three squatted on the gallery and ate, slowly, without talking; then in the store again, they drank from a tin dipper tepid water smelling of the cedar bucket and of living beech trees. And still they did not go home. It was a horse lot this time, a tall rail fence upon and along which men stood and sat and out of which one by one horses were led, to be walked and trotted and then cantered back and forth along the road while the slow swapping and buying went on and the sun began to slant westward, they – the three of them – watching and listening, the older brother with his muddy eyes and his steady, inevitable tobacco, the father commenting now and then on certain of the animals, to no one in particular.

It was after sundown when they reached home. They

---

ate supper by lamplight, then, sitting on the doorstep,
the boy watched the night fully accomplish, listening to
the whippoorwills and the frogs, when he heard his mother's voice: "Abner! No! No! Oh, God. Oh, God. Ab-
5 ner!" and he rose, whirled, and saw the altered light
through the door where a candle stub now burned in
a bottle neck on the table and his father, still in the
hat and coat, at once formal and burlesque as though
dressed carefully for some shabby and ceremonial vio-
10 lence, emptying the reservoir of the lamp back into the
five-gallon kerosene can from which it had been filled,
while the mother tugged at his arm until he shifted the
lamp to the other hand and flung her back, not sav-
agely or viciously, just hard, into the wall, her hands
15 flung out against the wall for balance, her mouth open
and in her face the same quality of hopeless despair as
had been in her voice. Then his father saw him standing
in the door.
"Go to the barn and get that can of oil we were oiling
20 the wagon with," he said. The boy did not move. Then
he could speak.
"What . . ." he cried. "What are you . . ."
"Go get that oil," his father said. "Go."
Then he was moving, running, outside the house, to-
25 ward the stable: this the old habit, the old blood which

---

6 **candle stub:** Kerzenstummel.
8 **burlesque:** grotesk.
9 **ceremonial:** feierlich.
10 **reservoir:** Behälter.
11 **five-gallon:** fünf Gallonen (*gallon:* Flüssigkeitsmaß; entspricht
   3,78 l).
   kerosene: Kerosin (Petroleum).
12 **to tug:** ziehen, zerren.

32

he had not been permitted to choose for himself, which
had been bequeathed him willy nilly and which had run
for so long (and who knew where, battening on what of
outrage and savagery and lust) before it came to him.
5   *I could keep on,* he thought. *I could run on and on and
never look back, never need to see his face again. Only
I can't. I can't,* the rusted can in his hand now, the liquid
sploshing in it as he ran back to the house and into it,
into the sound of his mother's weeping in the next
10 room, and handed the can to his father.
"Ain't you going to even send a nigger?" he cried. "At
least you sent a nigger before!"
This time his father didn't strike him. The hand came
even faster than the blow had, the same hand which
15 had set the can on the table with almost excruciating
care flashing from the can toward him too quick for
him to follow it, gripping him by the back of his shirt
and on to tiptoe before he had seen it quit the can, the
face stooping at him in breathless and frozen ferocity,
20 the cold, dead voice speaking over him to the older
brother who leaned against the table, chewing with that
steady, curious, sidewise motion of cows:
"Empty the can into the big one and go on. I'll catch up
with you."

---

2 **to bequeath s.th. to s.o.:** jdm. etwas vermachen.
   willy nilly: wohl oder übel.
3 **to batten on s.th.:** sich mit etwas mästen.
4 **outrage:** Wut, Empörung.
8 **to splosh:** schwappen.
15 **excruciating:** qualvoll.
16 **to flash:** sich blitzschnell bewegen.
18 **on to tiptoe:** auf Zehenspitzen.
   to quit: loslassen.

"Better tie him up to the bedpost," the brother said.

"Do like I told you," the father said. Then the boy was moving, his bunched shirt and the hard, bony hand between his shoulder-blades, his toes just touching the floor, across the room and into the other one, past the sisters sitting with spread heavy thighs in the two chairs over the cold hearth, and to where his mother and aunt sat side by side on the bed, the aunt's arms about his mother's shoulders.

"Hold him," the father said. The aunt made a startled movement. "Not you," the father said. "Lennie. Take hold of him. I want to see you do it." His mother took him by the wrist. "You'll hold him better than that. If he gets loose don't you know what he is going to do? He will go up yonder." He jerked his head toward the road. "Maybe I'd better tie him."

"I'll hold him," his mother whispered.

"See you do then." Then his father was gone, the stiff foot heavy and measured upon the boards, ceasing at last.

Then he began to struggle. His mother caught him in both arms, he jerking and wrenching at them. He would be stronger in the end, he knew that. But he had

---

1 **bedpost:** Bettpfosten.
3 **to bunch:** (zusammen)raffen.
  bony: knöchern, knochig.
4 **shoulder-blade:** Schulterblatt.
8 **side by side:** nebeneinander.
10 **startled:** erschrocken.
11 f. **to take hold of s.o.:** jdn. festhalten.
15 **yonder** (dial.): *beyond there.*
18 **See you do then:** Sieh zu, daß du's tust.
19 **measured:** rhythmisch; gemessen.
22 **to wrench:** reißen, zerren.

no time to wait for it. "Lemme go!" he cried. "I don't want to have to hit you!"

"Let him go!" the aunt said. "If he don't go, before God, I am going up there myself!"

5 "Don't you see I can't?" his mother cried. "Sarty! Sarty! No! No! Help me, Lizzie!"

Then he was free. His aunt grasped at him but it was too late. He whirled, running, his mother stumbled forward on to her knees behind him, crying to the nearer

10 sister: "Catch him, Net! Catch him!" But that was too late too, the sister (the sisters were twins, born at the same time, yet either of them now gave the impression of being, encompassing as much living meat and volume and weight as any other two of the family) not yet

15 having begun to rise from the chair, her head, face, alone merely turned, presenting to him in the flying instant an astonishing expanse of young female features untroubled by any surprise even, wearing only an expression of bovine interest. Then he was out of the

20 room, out of the house, in the mild dust of the starlit road and the heavy rifeness of honeysuckle, the pale ribbon unspooling with terrific slowness under his running feet, reaching the gate at last and turning in, running, his heart and lungs drumming, on up the drive to-

25 ward the lighted house, the lighted door. He did not knock, he burst in, sobbing for breath, incapable for the moment of speech; he saw the astonished face of

---

13 **to encompass:** einschließen, umfassen.
18 **untroubled:** hier: unberührt.
21 **rifeness:** Fülle.
22 **to unspool:** abspulen.
   terrific: schrecklich, fürchterlich.
26 **to sob:** schluchzen.

the Negro in the linen jacket without knowing when
the Negro had appeared.

"De Spain!" he cried, panted. "Where's ..." then he
saw the white man too emerging from a white door
down the hall. "Barn!" he cried. "Barn!"

"What?" the white man said. "Barn?"

"Yes!" the boy cried. "Barn!"

"Catch him!" the white man shouted.

But it was too late this time too. The Negro grasped his
shirt, but the entire sleeve, rotten with washing, carried
away, and he was out that door too and in the drive
again, and had actually never ceased to run even while
he was screaming into the white man's face.

Behind him the white man was shouting, "My horse!
Fetch my horse!" and he thought for an instant of cut-
ting across the park and climbing the fence into the
road, but he did not know the park nor how high the
vine-massed fence might be and he dared not risk it. So
he ran on down the drive, blood and breath roaring;
presently he was in the road again though he could not
see it. He could not hear either: the galloping mare was
almost upon him before he heard her, and even then he
held his course, as if the very urgency of his wild grief
and need must in a moment more find him wings, waiting until the ultimate instant to hurl himself aside and
into the weed-choked roadside ditch as the horse thun-

---

3 **to pant:** keuchen.

10 **rotten:** zerschlissen.

10 f. **to carry away:** hier: nachgeben.

15 f. **to cut across s.th.:** quer durch etwas laufen.

18 **vine-massed:** von Ranken überwuchert.

25 **to hurl o.s. aside:** sich zur Seite werfen.

26 **weed-choked:** voller Unkraut.

dered past and on, for an instant in furious silhouette
against the stars, the tranquil early summer night sky
which, even before the shape of the horse and rider
vanished, stained abruptly and violently upward: a
5 long, swirling roar incredible and soundless, blotting
the stars, and he springing up and into the road again,
running again, knowing it was too late yet still running
even after he heard the shot and, an instant later, two
shots, pausing now without knowing he had ceased to
10 run, crying "Pap! Pap!", running again before he knew
he had begun to run, stumbling, tripping over something and scrabbling up again without ceasing to run,
looking backward over his shoulder at the glare as he
got up, running on among the invisible trees, panting,
15 sobbing, "Father! Father!"
At midnight he was sitting on the crest of a hill. He did
not know it was midnight and he did not know how far
he had come. But there was no glare behind him now
and he sat now, his back toward what he had called
20 home for four days anyhow, his face toward the dark
woods which he would enter when breath was strong
again, small, shaking steadily in the chill darkness, hug-
ging himself into the remainder of his thin, rotten shirt,

---

2 **tranquil:** ruhig.
4 **to stain:** sich verfärben.
   abruptly (adv.): plötzlich.
5 **to swirl:** wirbeln.
   to blot: auslöschen.
13 **glare:** Feuerschein.
14 **invisible:** unsichtbar.
16 **crest:** (Berg-)Kuppe.
22 **chill:** kühl.
22 f. **to hug o.s.:** hier: sich kuscheln, schmiegen.
23 **remainder:** Rest.

the grief and despair now no longer terror and fear but just grief and despair. *Father. My father,* he thought. "He was brave!" he cried suddenly, aloud but not loud, no more than a whisper: "He was! He was in the war!
5 He was in Colonel Sartoris' cav'ry!" not knowing that his father had gone to that war a private in the fine old European sense, wearing no uniform, admitting the authority of and giving fidelity to no man or army or flag, going to war as Malbrouck[6] himself did: for booty – it
10 meant nothing and less than nothing to him if it were enemy booty or his own.
The slow constellations wheeled on. It would be dawn and then sun-up after a while and he would be hungry. But that would be to-morrow and now he was only
15 cold, and walking would cure that. His breathing was easier now and he decided to get up and go on, and then he found that he had been asleep because he knew it was almost dawn, the night almost over. He could tell that from the whippoorwills. They were everywhere
20 now among the dark trees below him, constant and inflectioned and ceaseless, so that, as the instant for giving over to the day birds drew nearer and nearer, there was no interval at all between them. He got up. He was a little stiff, but walking would cure that too as it would

---

5 **cav'ry** (dial.): *cavalry:* Kavallerie.
6 **private:** gemeiner Soldat.
8 **fidelity:** Treue.
9 **booty:** Beute.
12 **constellation:** Sternbild.
13 **sun-up:** Sonnenaufgang.
20 f. **inflectioned:** hier: abgewandelt.
21 f. **to give over to s.th.:** einer Sache weichen, sich einer Sache ergeben.

the cold, and soon there would be the sun. He went on down the hill, toward the dark woods within which the liquid silver voices of the birds called unceasing – the rapid and urgent beating of the urgent and quiring
5 heart of the late spring night. He did not look back.

---

3 **liquid:** hier: klar, hell.
4 **to quire** (arch.): im Chor singen.

Editorische Notiz

Der englische Text folgt der Ausgabe: William Faulkner, *Collected Stories*, New York: Random House, 1950, S. 3–25. Das Glossar erklärt in der Regel alle Wörter, die nicht in *Reclams Englischem Wörterbuch* von Dieter Hamblock (Stuttgart: Reclam, 1996) verzeichnet sind.

Im Glossar verwendete Abkürzungen

adv.	adverb
arch.	archaic (veraltet)
dial.	dialectal (mundartlich)
fig.	figuratively (übertragen)
o.s.	oneself
pl.	plural
s.o.	someone
s.th.	something

Anmerkungen

1 Anspielung auf zwei weitverbreitete Konservenmarken, deren eine eine kleine Teufelsfigur, die andere einen springenden Fisch auf dem Etikett trugen. In den Dosen befand sich konserviertes Fleisch bzw. eingelegter Fisch.

2 Wie Faulkner in dem Roman *The Unvanquished* erzählt, war Ab Snopes, selbst ein Südstaatler, im Krieg zwischen den Nord- und den Südstaaten (1861–65) zeitweise damit beschäftigt, Pferde von den kämpfenden Truppen, auch von den eigenen, zu stehlen. Vgl. S. 38 sowie Anm. 3 und 5. – Durch den Hinweis auf den drei Jahrzehnte zurückliegenden Vorfall datiert Faulkner die Ereignisse von »Barn Burning« auf die erste Hälfte der neunziger Jahre des 19. Jh.s.

3 Die Uniformen der Konföderierten Armee waren grau, die der Truppen der Nordstaaten blau.

4 Ab Snopes ist ein »share cropper«, d. h. er pachtet Land auf der Basis von Anteilen (»shares«) an der Ernte (»crop«), die der Landbesitzer (»landlord«) am Ende des Jahres einbehält. Vermutl. gehört er zu der Gruppe von Pächtern (»tenants«), die in jeder Hinsicht von ihren Landbesitzern abhängig waren und von diesen neben dem Land und der Unterkunft – gewöhnlich einem einfachen Haus – auch die landwirtschaftlichen Geräte sowie das Saatgut zur Verfügung gestellt bekamen. Dafür mußten sie am Ende der Saison in der Regel die Hälfte der eingebrachten Ernte abliefern. Einzelheiten wurden in einem Pachtvertrag (»contract«) geregelt. Wie dem Text zu entnehmen ist, hielt es Snopes nie länger als eine Saison bei einem Pachtherrn aus.

5 de Spain, Snopes' Pachtherr, will Snopes als Ersatz für die beschädigte Teppichbrücke 20 Scheffel Mais in Rechnung stellen, die dieser zusätzlich zu dem im Vertrag vereinbarten Anteil der Ernte abzuliefern hat. Snopes soll den geänderten Vertrag bei seinem nächsten Gang zum »commissary«

unterschreiben. Wegen dieser Änderung des Vertrages verklagt Snopes de Spain vor Gericht. – Der »commissary« ist ein vom Land- oder Plantagenbesitzer geführter Laden, in dem die Pächter ihre Lebensmittel, Kleidung u. ä. auf Kredit erhielten. Die am Ende des Jahres ausstehenden Gelder wurden gegen die Ernte verrechnet. Es stand dem Landbesitzer frei, für die dem Pächter auf Kredit überlassenen Waren Zinsen zu fordern. Viele Pächter kamen auf diese Weise nie zu Bargeld.

6 Herzog von Marlborough (1650–1722), englischer Feldherr, dem nachgesagt wurde, daß er sich in seinen Feldzügen an Freund und Feind persönlich bereicherte. Die Wendung »a private in the fine old European sense« (Z. 6) ist dahingehend zu verstehen, daß ein als »private« bezeichneter Mann kein öffentliches Amt bekleidete und nur seinen eigenen Zwecken diente.

Literaturhinweise

I. *Bibliographien*

Basset, John E., *William Faulkner: An Annotated Checklist of Criticism*, New York 1972.
- *Faulkner: An Annotated Checklist of Recent Criticism*, Kent (Ohio) 1983.
- *Faulkner in the Eighties: An Annotated Critical Bibliography*, Metuchen (N. J.) 1991.

Sixteen Modern American Authors, Bd. 2: *A Survey of Research and Criticism Since 1972*, hrsg. von Jackson R. Bryer, Durham (N. C.) 1990, S. 210–300.

II. *Biographien*

Blotner, Joseph, *Faulkner: A Biography*, 2 Bde., New York 1974.
- *Faulkner: A Biography*, überarb. Aufl., New York 1984.
Nicolaisen, Peter, *William Faulkner in Selbstzeugnissen und Bilddokumenten*, Reinbek b. Hamburg [3]1995 ([1]1981).

III. *Sekundärliteratur*

Billingslea, Oliver, »Fathers and Sons: The Spiritual Quest in Faulkner's ›Barn Burning‹«, in: *Mississippi Quarterly* 44 (1991) S. 287–308.
Bradford, M. E., »Family and Community in Faulkner's ›Barn Burning‹«, in: *Southern Review* 17 (1981) S. 332–339.
Buschendorf, Christa, *Mit Kinderaugen: Zur Perspektivtechnik bei William Faulkner, Carson McCullers und Flannery O'Connor*, Würzburg 1987.
Cacket, Kathy, »›Barn Burning‹: Debating the American Adam«, in: *Notes on Mississippi Writers* 21 (1989) S. 1–17.

Carothers, James B., *William Faulkner's Short Stories*, Ann Arbor (Mich.) 1985.

Comprone, Joseph, »Literature and the Writing Process: A Pedagogical Reading of ›Barn Burning‹«, in: *College Literature* 9 (1982) S. 1–21.

Crocker, Michael W. / Evans, Robert C., »Faulkner's ›Barn Burning‹ and Flannery O'Connor's ›Everything That Rises Must Converge‹«, in: *College Language Association Journal* 36 (1992) S. 371–383.

Fisher, Marvin, »The World of Faulkner's Children«, in: *University of Kansas City Review* 27 (1960/62) S. 13–18.

Fowler, Virginia C., »Faulkner's ›Barn Burning‹: Sarty's Conflict Reconsidered«, in: *College Language Association Journal* 24 (1982) S. 513–522.

Franklin, Phyllis, »Sarty Snopes and ›Barn Burning‹«, in: *Mississippi Quarterly* 21 (1968) S. 189–193.

Hall, Joan Wylie, »Faulkner's Barn Burners: Ab Snopes and the Duke of Marlborough«, in: *Notes on Mississippi Writers* 21 (1989) S. 65–68.

Harrington, Evans / Abadie, Ann J. (Hrsg.), *Faulkner and the Short Story: Faulkner and Yoknapatawpha 1990*, Jackson (Miss.) 1992.

Hiles, Jane, »Kinship and Heredity in Faulkner's ›Barn Burning‹«, in: *Mississippi Quarterly* 38 (1985) S. 329–337.

Hoffmann, Gerhard, »Die Rolle des Ich-Erzählers in Faulkners Kurzgeschichten«, in: *Archiv für das Studium der Neueren Sprachen* 201 (1964/65) S. 339–349.

Hoffmann, Gisela, »Faulkner: ›Barn Burning‹«, in: *Die amerikanische Kurzgeschichte*, hrsg. von Karl Heinz Göller und Gerhard Hoffmann, Düsseldorf 1972, S. 258–267, 413 f.

Howell, Elmo, »Colonel Sartoris Snopes and Faulkner's Aristocrats: A Note on ›Barn Burning‹«, in: *The Carolina Quarterly* 11 (1958/59) S. 13–19.

Johnston, Kenneth G., »Time of Decline: Pickett's Charge and the Broken Clock in Faulkner's ›Barn Burning‹«, in: *Studies in Short Fiction* 11 (1974) S. 434–436.

Millgate, Michael, *The Achievement of William Faulkner*, New York 1966.

Mitchell, Charles, »The Wounded Will of Faulkner's Barn Burner«, in: *Modern Fiction Studies* 11 (1965) S. 185–189.

Moreland, Richard C., *Faulkner and Modernism: Rereading and Rewriting*, Madison (Wisc.) 1990.

Nicolaisen, Peter, »Hemingways ›My Old Man‹ und Faulkners ›Barn Burning‹: Ein Vergleich«, in: *Amerikanische Erzählungen von Hawthorne bis Salinger: Interpretationen*, hrsg. von Paul G. Buchloh [u. a.], Neumünster 1968, S. 187–223.

Rio-Jelliffe, R., »The Language of Time in Fiction: A Model in Faulkner's ›Barn Burning‹«, in: *Journal of Narrative Technique* 24 (1994) S. 98–113.

Skaggs, Merill Maguire, »Story and Film in ›Barn Burning‹: The Difference a Camera Makes«, in: *Southern Quarterly* 21 (1983) S. 5–15.

Skei, Hans, *William Faulkner: The Short Story Career. An Outline of Faulkner's Short Story Writing from 1919–1962*, Oslo 1981.

– *William Faulkner: The Novelist as Short Story Writer*, Oslo 1985.

Stein, William B., »Faulkner's Devil«, in: *Modern Language Notes* 56 (1961) S. 731 f.

Volpe, Edmond L., »›Barn Burning‹: A Definition of Evil«, in: *Faulkner: The Unappeased Imagination*, hrsg. von Glenn O. Carey, Troy (N. Y.) 1980, S. 75–82.

Wilson, Gayle E., »›Being Pulled Two Ways‹: The Nature of Sarty's Choice in ›Barn Burning‹«, in: *Mississippi Quarterly* 24 (1971) S. 279–288.

Yunis, S. Susan, »The Narrator of Faulkner's ›Barn Burning‹«, in: *Faulkner Journal* 6 (1991) S. 23–31.

Zender, Karl F., »Character and Symbol in ›Barn Burning‹«, in: *College Literature* 16 (1989) S. 48–59.

Ziegler, Heide, *Die existentielle Erzählweise als Strukturprinzip kurzen Erzählens. Das Komische, Tragische, Groteske und Mythische in William Faulkners Short Stories*, Stuttgart 1977.

Nachwort

»Yoknapatawpha County« hat Faulkner das Gebiet genannt, in dem die meisten seiner Erzählungen und Romane angesiedelt sind. Es liegt im nördlichen Teil des Staates Mississippi und entspricht bis in Einzelheiten der Gegend, in der der Autor aufwuchs und den größten Teil seines Lebens verbrachte. Der Name ist indianischen Ursprungs. Auf einer selbstgezeichneten Landkarte hat Faulkner sich als »sole owner and proprietor« dieses fiktiven Landstrichs bezeichnet und später, im Rückblick auf sein erzählerisches Werk, davon gesprochen, daß er sich seinen eigenen »Kosmos« erschaffen habe:

> »Beginning with *Sartoris* I discovered that my own little postage stamp of native soil was worth writing about and that I would never live long enough to exhaust it, and that by sublimating the actual into the apocryphal I would have complete liberty to use whatever talent I might have to its absolute top. It opened up a gold mine of other people, so I created a cosmos of my own.«[1]

Geboren am 25. September 1897, begann Faulkner seine literarische Laufbahn, nach unregelmäßigem Schulbesuch und einer kurzen Zeit als Kadett in der Royal Air Force in Kanada, mit lyrischen Veröffentlichungen. Er schloß Freundschaft mit dem Romancier Sherwood Anderson, begab sich auf eine Europareise

---

1 James B. Meriwether / Michael Millgate (Hrsg.), *Lion in the Garden: Interviews with William Faulkner 1926–1962*, New York: Random House, 1968, S. 255.

und machte seine ersten, noch tastenden Versuche als Erzähler. Dann folgt fast unvermittelt eine Phase kaum vorstellbarer Schaffenskraft. In einem Zeitraum von nur zwei Jahren entstehen vier große Romane: *Sartoris* (1929), *The Sound and the Fury* (1929), *As I Lay Dying* (1930) und *Sanctuary* (1931). Sie erzählen von schwierigen Verhältnissen zwischen Kindern und Eltern, Brüdern und Schwestern, Familiengeschichten also, die in die Geschichte der Südstaaten eingebettet sind. Das Geschehen vollzieht sich gewöhnlich vor einem ländlichen, bisweilen auch kleinstädtischen Hintergrund. Die Darstellungsweise ist kompliziert. Wie viele seiner Zeitgenossen experimentierte Faulkner mit verschiedenen Techniken des »Bewußtseinsstroms« und des »inneren Monologs«; er war an der subjektiven Wahrnehmung der Welt interessiert. Seine Charaktere, ob Männer oder Frauen, tun sich schwer damit, ihre Existenz zu akzeptieren. Sie leiden unter ihrer Sexualität und empfinden das Leben als schmerzhaft, suchen nach Gerechtigkeit und Sinn und verzweifeln nicht selten an der Ordnung der Welt, in die sie hineingeboren sind. Aus solchem Gefühl heraus stürzt sich Bayard Sartoris in dem Roman *Sartoris* mit einem Flugzeug in den Tod. Eine der Figuren in *The Sound and the Fury*, deren Wahrnehmungen, Erinnerungen und Empfindungen Faulkner wiedergibt, ist schwachsinnig; eine andere begeht Selbstmord. In *Sanctuary* ist von sexueller Perversion die Rede; *As I Lay Dying* stellt mit großer Eindringlichkeit Gefühle der Isolation und Fremdheit dar. Später sprach Faulkner von dem Gefühl der Ekstase, das er beim Schreiben von *The Sound and the Fury* empfunden habe:

»[...] that ecstasy, that eager and joyous faith and anticipation of surprise which the yet unmarred sheet beneath my hand held inviolate and unfailing, waiting for release.«[2]

Er schrieb mit Leidenschaft, seines künstlerischen Weges sicher und ohne Rücksicht auf die möglichen Erwartungen seiner Leser: »One day I seemed to shut a door between me and all publishers' addresses and book lists. I said to myself, Now I can write.«[3]

Faulkner heiratete, gründete eine Familie und erwarb Haus- und Grundbesitz in der kleinen Stadt Oxford im Norden Mississippis, die in seinen Romanen als »Jefferson« erscheint. Zu den Rollen, die er gern spielte, gehörte die des Farmers; später gab er sich mit Vorliebe wie ein Aristokrat aus der Zeit des alten Südens. Sein Haus in Oxford stammte aus der Zeit vor dem Bürgerkrieg. Offenbar drängte es ihn, sich mit dem Süden zu identifizieren, zugleich aber war und blieb er ein Künstler, der sich allein seinem Werk verpflichtet fühlte. Aus finanziellen Gründen verdingte er sich als Drehbuchautor in Hollywood, kehrte aber immer wieder nach Oxford zurück.

In den zahlreichen Kurzgeschichten und Romanen, die in den dreißiger Jahren entstanden, gewinnen Yoknapatawpha County und der Ort Jefferson geographische, soziale, vor allem auch historische Konturen. *Light in August* (1932) und *Absalom, Absalom!* (1936) handeln, in unterschiedlicher Weise, vom Rassenkonflikt, den Faulkner, wie andere vor und nach ihm, als

---

2 W. Faulkner, »An Introduction to *The Sound and the Fury*«, in: W. F., *The Sound and the Fury*, hrsg. von David Minter, New York: Norton, 1987, S. 218–220, hier S. 219.

3 Ebd., S. 220.

einen auf den Südstaaten lastenden Fluch bezeichnet hat. Joe Christmas, der Protagonist des Romans *Light in August*, verzweifelt daran, daß er nicht weiß, ob er zu den Schwarzen oder den Weißen gehört. Er wird von einem Mob gelyncht, nachdem er eine weiße Frau umgebracht hat. Diese, eine Nachfahrin von Abolitionisten, hatte sich ihm hingegeben und ihn bedrängt, sich als Schwarzer zu bekennen – in seinem Tod wird ihm seine Identität gleichsam diktiert. In *Absalom, Absalom!* tötet ein Mann seinen Halbbruder, dessen Mutter eine Mulattin war; hier vermischt sich das Motiv des Rassenkonflikts mit dem des Inzests, das schon in *Sartoris* und *The Sound and the Fury* von zentraler Bedeutung ist. Wiederum rückt Faulkner die Form des Erzählens in den Vordergrund – es geht ihm um die Frage, wie wir Geschichte (und Geschichten) erfahren und in unserem Bewußtsein rekonstruieren, um Formen der Überlieferung und das Problem der Wahrheitsfindung. Einer der Erzähler des Romans ist Quentin Compson, eine Figur aus *The Sound and the Fury*, die unverkennbar autobiographische Züge trägt. Auf die Frage: »Why do you hate the South?«, die ihm am Ende des Romans gestellt wird, antwortet Quentin:

> »I dont hate it,‹ Quentin said, quickly, at once, immediately; ›I dont hate it‹, he said. *I dont hate it* he thought, panting in the cold air, the iron New England dark: *I dont. I dont! I dont hate it! I dont hate it!*«[4]

Absalom, Absalom! ist zum Teil in Hollywood entstanden, zu einem Zeitpunkt, als der Tod seines jüngsten

4 W. Faulkner, *Novels 1936–1940*, hrsg. von Joseph Blotner und Noel Polk, New York: The Library of America, 1990, S. 311.

Bruders, der bei einem Flugzeugabsturz ums Leben gekommen war, den Autor tief erschütterte. Wie oft in
seinem Leben flüchtete Faulkner sich in den Rausch.
Nach *Pylon*(1935), *The Unvanquished* (1938) und *The
Wild Palms* (1939) folgte gegen Ende des Jahrzehnts
mit *The Hamlet* (1940) der erste Teil einer Trilogie über
die Geschichte der Familie Snopes, in deren Umkreis
auch die Erzählung »Barn Burning« gehört. Faulkner
war von dem Rang seines neuen Buches überzeugt; in
einem Brief an seinen Verleger vermerkte er, fast bei-
läufig und in einem Nachsatz: »I am the best in America, by God.«[5] Der Stoff hatte ihn schon in seinen An-
fängen als Schriftsteller beschäftigt; ein Fragment mit
dem Titel *Father Abraham* geht in das Jahr 1926 zurück. An diesem Stoff arbeitete er von jetzt ab, wenn
auch mit großen Unterbrechungen, bis nahezu an sein
Lebensende. Der zweite Teil der Trilogie, *The Town*,
erschien im Jahre 1957; zwei Jahre später schließlich
der letzte Band *The Mansion*.
Schon zu seinen Lebzeiten galt Faulkner als schwieri-
ger Autor, und Mitte der vierziger Jahre war von seinen Büchern mit der Ausnahme von *Sanctuary* kein
einziges lieferbar, nicht einmal der Band *Go Down,
Moses* (1942), der – neben dem Thema der Sklaverei
und ihrer Folgen – vor allem die Frage nach dem Recht
des Menschen auf Land- und Grundbesitz behandelt.
In *Intruder in the Dust* (1947) griff Faulkner die Ras-
senthematik erneut auf. Mit der Verfilmung dieses Romans und insbesondere nach der Auszeichnung des
Autors mit dem Nobelpreis verbreitete sich sein Ruhm,
und Faulkner meldete sich nun zunehmend, im Inland

5 W. Faulkner, *Selected Letters*, hrsg. von Joseph Blotner, New York: Random House, 1977, S. 113.

wie im Ausland, öffentlich zu literarischen, politischen und gesellschaftlichen Fragen zu Wort. Seine Stellungnahmen zur Rassentrennung waren kontrovers und entfremdeten ihn zeitweilig sowohl von seinen Mitbürgern im Süden wie von den liberalen Nordstaatlern. Nach *Requiem for a Nun* (1951) erschien im Jahre 1954 mit *A Fable* sein einziger Roman, der nicht auf die Südstaaten Bezug nimmt. Er spielt in Frankreich und handelt von der Meuterei eines Regiments im Ersten Weltkrieg, die fast zu einem Waffenstillstand der kämpfenden Mächte geführt hätte. Das Bild des Menschen, das der Roman entwirft, ist düster und läßt wenig Raum für den Optimismus, mit dem Faulkner in seiner Nobelpreisrede die literarische Welt überrascht hatte. In seinem letzten, wie in einer Stimmung heiterer Wehmut geschriebenen Roman *The Reivers* (1962) kehrte Faulkner noch einmal in die Welt Yoknapatawphas und deren Vergangenheit zurück. Er starb am 6. Juni 1962 in seinem Heimatort Oxford (Mississippi).

Die Geschichte »Barn Burning« ist im Spätherbst des Jahres 1938 in gerade zehn Tagen entstanden, ein Zeichen dafür, wie sicher sich der Autor seiner erzählerischen Kraft und des Stoffes war. Ursprünglich als Einleitungskapitel für den Roman *The Hamlet* gedacht, wurde der Text als selbständige Erzählung im Juni 1939 in *Harper's Magazine* veröffentlicht und wenig später mit dem zum ersten Mal vergebenen »O. Henry Memorial Award« als beste Kurzgeschichte des Jahres ausgezeichnet. Neben dem bereits erwähnten Stoffkreis um die Familie Snopes läßt Faulkner die Geschichte einer weiteren Familie anklingen. Der Vorname des jugendlichen Protagonisten, Colonel Sartoris,

weist auf einen der bedeutenden Männer in der gleich-
namigen Familie hin, über deren Schicksal die Romane
Sartoris und *The Unvanquished* berichten. Während
die Snopes' überwiegend arme, kaum des Lesens und
Schreibens kundige Landpächter sind, gehören die Sartoris' zur Aristokratie der Südstaaten; sie sind reiche
Landbesitzer und blicken voller Stolz auf eine lange
Familientradition zurück. Auf den im Bürgerkrieg er-
worbenen Ruhm des Colonels spielt der Friedensrich-
ter an, wenn er sagt: »I reckon anybody named for Colonel Sartoris in this country can't help but tell the
truth, can they?« (S. 5). An dem Beispiel wird sichtbar,
wie eng miteinander verflochten die Werke Faulkners
sind. In der Tat bilden sie einen eigenen »Kosmos«,
eine Welt, über die der Autor frei verfügte und in der
er die Fäden spann, die sich zwischen den Bewohnern
und ihren Geschichten ergaben.
Mit der Verbindung der Namen Snopes und Sartoris
deutet Faulkner den Konflikt an, in dem sich der Junge
in »Barn Burning« befindet. Sarty fühlt sich eng an seinen Vater gebunden, ist stolz auf ihn und bewundert
ihn, sehnt sich aber zugleich nach einer anderen Le-
bensweise als jener, die der Vater sich selbst und seiner
Familie aufzwingt. Dessen unbedingtem Willen, sich
anderen gegenüber zu behaupten – »that ravening and
jealous rage« (S. 16), heißt es im Text – steht der
Wunsch des Kindes nach einem Leben in »peace and
dignity« (S. 15) gegenüber, wie es in seinen Augen
Haus und Anwesen de Spains verkörpern. Der Junge
fühlt sich wie von zwei in unterschiedliche Richtungen
wirkenden Kräften hin und her gezogen (»being pulled
two ways like between two teams of horses«, S. 26) und
träumt davon, daß sich die Spannung, unter der er lei-

det, lösen möge. Indem er de Spain von dem erneuten Brandanschlag des Vaters unterrichtet, wendet er sich am Ende gegen das väterliche Erbe. Aber er liebt und verehrt den Vater nach wie vor; nach seiner Entscheidung empfindet er »grief and despair«. Wohin ihn sein Weg führt, bleibt offen.

Es lohnt sich, den Loyalitätskonflikt, dem sich Sarty ausgesetzt sieht, näher zu betrachten. Wo der Junge, übermannt von einer Woge des Gefühls (»a surge of peace and joy«, S. 14), »dignity« sieht, erkennt der Vater Reichtum, der sich auf die Arbeit und Ausbeutung anderer gründet: »That's sweat. Nigger sweat. Maybe it ain't white enough yet to suit him. Maybe he wants to mix some white sweat with it« (S. 19), sagt Ab Snopes. Er glaubt sich dem Pachtherrn mit Leib und Seele ausgeliefert (»I'll have a word with the man that aims to begin to-morrow owning me body and soul for the next eight months«, S. 13) und versucht, seinen Sohn über die Ungerechtigkeit eines Systems zu belehren, das Landbesitzer wie de Spain (oder Sartoris) zu fast unumschränkten Herrschern über ihre Pächter macht. Freilich fällt es dem Leser nicht leicht, für Ab Snopes Partei zu ergreifen. Faulkner zeichnet ihn als eine zwielichtige Figur, die zu Gewalttätigkeit neigt und sich über Recht und Gerechtigkeit hinwegsetzt. Überdies ist Ab Snopes faul, ein Brandstifter und Pferdedieb, dessen Verhalten im Bürgerkrieg alles andere als tapfer und ehrenhaft war. Damals hielt er sich zwischen den Fronten auf und kämpfte allein für seinen eigenen, privaten Vorteil.

Ungeachtet seines zweifelhaften Charakters ist Snopes' Kritik an dem System des »tenant farming« und »share cropping« nicht unberechtigt (vgl. oben S. 43, Anm. 4).

Diese Form der Landwirtschaft war nach dem Ende des Bürgerkrieges in den Südstaaten an die Stelle der alten, auf die Sklaverei gestützten Plantagenwirtschaft getreten und regelte die Beziehungen zwischen Landbesitzern und Pächtern – gewöhnlich zu Gunsten der ersteren. Die in der Erzählung geschilderten Ereignisse tragen sich im letzten Jahrzehnt des 19. Jahrhunderts zu; damals wie noch in der Entstehungszeit von »Barn Burning« waren die sozialen Unterschiede zwischen den armen Pächtern und den wohlhabenden Landbesitzern erheblich. De Spains Verhalten ist typisch: Selbstherrlich setzt er die »Strafe« für Snopes fest und kann es nicht glauben, daß sein Pächter gegen ihn vor Gericht zieht. Doch auch in anderer Hinsicht dürfte er die Bewunderung, die Sarty angesichts seines herrschaftlichen Hauses empfindet, kaum verdienen. In der Auseinanderstzung mit Snopes wirkt er schwach, gerät außer sich vor Zorn und scheint vor allem deswegen gegen seinen Pächter vorzugehen, weil seine Frau es so will. Über Mrs. de Spain aber erfahren wir nur, daß sie wegen eines beschmutzten Teppichs in hysterische Klagen ausbricht. Von einer neutralen Warte aus betrachtet, hat die Erzählung durchaus komische Züge.

Der Junge Sarty, aus dessen Sicht wir die Ereignisse erleben, kann die Komik des Geschehens freilich nicht empfinden. Wenn er sich sowohl im Blick auf seinen Vater wie auf de Spain von falschen Vorstellungen leiten läßt, so unterstreicht dies nur seine Hilflosigkeit, von der in der Erzählung mehrfach die Rede ist. Immer wieder mißversteht er die Vorgänge, die sich um ihn herum zutragen, und selbst dann, wenn ihm der Vater etwas erklärt, teilt sich ihm nur die eigene Befangenheit mit: »divulging nothing to him save the terrible handicap of being young, the light weight of his few years« (S. 13). Ein kühles Abwägen zwischen verschiedenen Möglichkeiten ist ihm schon auf Grund seiner Jugend nicht möglich; noch schwerer dürfte ihm die Entscheidung fallen, weil seine Bindung an den Vater rational kaum faßbar ist. Faulkner spricht von »den Banden des Blutes«, die der Junge fühlt (»the old fierce pull of blood«, S. 3; »the old blood which he had not been permitted to choose for himself«, S. 32 f.), und betont, daß der Entschluß, den Vater zu verraten, plötzlich und eher intuitiv erfolgt. Noch Jahre später denkt Sarty über sein Verhalten nach: »Later, twenty years later, he was to tell himself [. . .]« (S. 12). Wird dem Erwachsenen bewußt, daß er als Kind mit dem Verrat des Vaters zumindest indirekt ein höchst fragwürdiges Wirtschaftssystem sanktioniert hat?

Die Frage erhält zusätzliches Gewicht, wenn man sich vergegenwärtigt, daß in »Barn Burning« in leichter Abwandlung eine Szene wiederholt wird, die in Faulkners großem Roman *Absalom, Absalom!* eine das Geschehen entscheidende Wende auslöst. Dort berichtet der spätere Plantagenbesitzer Thomas Sutpen, daß er als Kind eines armen Landpächters unter ähnlichen Umständen wie Ab Snopes durch einen schwarzen Sklaven von der Schwelle des prachtvollen Hauses verwiesen wurde, in dem der mächtige Landbesitzer wohnte – damals habe er sich geschworen, einst selbst ein reicher Pflanzer zu werden und so die Tradition des alten Südens fortzusetzen. Sutpen scheitert, und mit dem Ende des Bürgerkrieges scheint in *Absalom, Absalom!* ein für allemal auch das Ende der alten, »aristokratischen« Lebensform der Südstaaten gekommen zu sein. In »Barn Burning« greift Faulkner die Szene abermals auf, Sarty allerdings reagiert auf die Zurückweisung des Vaters von der Schwelle de Spains kaum. Anders als Sutpen will sich Ab Snopes gegen das herrschende System behaupten, der Sohn aber sucht einen Kompromiß. Als Erwachsener wird er im Spruch des Gerichts das Bemühen um »truth, justice« (S. 12) sehen – ist dies vielleicht die Stellung, die Faulkner im Jahre 1938, als er »Barn Burning« schrieb, zur Geschichte des Südens beziehen möchte?

Einerlei, ob man eher die Seite des Jungen oder die des Vaters betont, es wird rasch klar, wie vielschichtig die Erzählung »Barn Burning« ist. Entsprechend unterschiedlich sind deren Interpretationen ausgefallen, ja wenn man will, kann man an ihnen die Geschichte der Faulkner-Kritik ablesen. Wurde zunächst einer Lesart der Vorzug gegeben, derzufolge Faulkner in »Barn Burning« die »alte Ordnung« des Südens gegen den aufstrebenden »Snopsismus« verteidigte, ist man heute eher geneigt, den Autor für die Position Ab Snopes' zu reklamieren, wie denn in den letzten Jahren die Figur des Vaters immer stärker in den Vordergrund der Deutung gerückt ist. Aber auch an psychologischen Auslegungen des Textes hat es nicht gefehlt. So ist »Barn Burning« als ein Beispiel für den in der amerikanischen Literatur häufigen Typus der »Initiationsgeschichte« verstanden worden; noch weiter gehen jene Kritiker, die im Sinne Freuds in Sartys Verrat des Vaters eine Art oedipalen Vatermord sehen. Schließlich ergeben sich unter dem Eindruck der feministischen Literaturkritik neue Fragestellungen. Geht es in »Barn Burning« nicht auch um eine Auseinandersetzung zwischen männlichem und weiblichem Rollenverhalten? Letzteres wird nicht nur im »hysteric [...] woman-wail« Mrs.

de Spains, sondern auch in den Schwestern Sartys deutlich karikiert. Zugleich aber läßt Faulkner den Jungen gemeinsam mit den Frauen schützende Umzäunungen für die Tiere bauen. Man hat gemeint, daß der Autor hierin der zerstörerischen männlichen Selbstbehauptung ein anderes, eher weibliches Prinzip gegenüberstellt; in der Tat schwört der Sohn durch den Verrat des Vaters nicht zuletzt dessen Gewalttätigkeit ab. In diesem Verhalten ähnelt er anderen Helden Faulkners, insbesondere Bayard Sartoris in dem Roman *The Unvanquished*, der kurz vor »Barn Burning« erschienen war. Auch Bayard verzichtet als junger Mann darauf, die Tradition seiner Familie fortzusetzen, in der es gerade in Fragen der Ehre oft zu gewalttätigen Auseinandersetzungen gekommen ist.

Die Ähnlichkeiten zwischen der Erzählung »Barn Burning« und anderen Werken Faulkners sind jedoch nicht allein im thematischen Bereich begründet; sie finden sich vor allem auch in der dem Autor eigenen Darstellungsweise. Typisch ist der Gebrauch der Perspektivtechnik. Zwar kommentiert der Erzähler gelegentlich die Wahrnehmungen des Jungen oder formuliert dessen Empfindungen wie ein Älterer, der dem sprachlich noch unbeholfenen Kind nachhelfen muß, meistens aber ist es Faulkner vorrangig um die Subjektivität der wiedergegebenen Erfahrung zu tun. Der einleitende Abschnitt liefert ein deutliches Beispiel. Er ist geprägt von den gegenwärtigen Wahrnehmungen des Kindes. Der Raum, in dem es sich befindet, wirkt bedrängend, sinnliche Eindrücke stürzen auf den Jungen ein, ohne daß er sich ihrer erwehren oder sie kontrollieren könnte. Dabei schildert Faulkner weniger, was Sarty sieht, hört oder riecht, als vielmehr den Prozeß der

Wahrnehmung und die Art und Weise, wie er die Umwelt erfährt. Er stellt dar, wie sich sinnliche Reize mit anderen Empfindungen verbinden, und spricht insbesondere von der Wirkung der Dinge auf den Betrachter. Das unmittelbare Erlebnis der Welt wird zum Ziel der Gestaltung – eben darum ist die Syntax Faulkners oftmals so kompliziert. »Deluged as though by a warm wave by a suave turn of carpeted stair and a pendant glitter of chandeliers and a mute gleam of golden frames« (S. 17), heißt es, als Sarty das Innere des de Spainschen Hauses sieht. Ähnlich wie bei Joseph Conrad, von dem Faulkner deutlich beeinflußt war, richtet sich die Darstellung weniger auf das Objekt selbst als auf die Qualitäten, die von ihm auszugehen scheinen. Die Attribute der Dinge verselbständigen sich und nehmen den Menschen gefangen; sie bedrängen ihn und rücken die Welt so nahe an ihn heran, daß er sich ihrer nicht entziehen kann. Man beachte, wie oft Sarty körperlichen Berührungen ausgesetzt ist und wie häufig er geradezu gebannt nur auf das unmittelbar vor ihm Liegende starrt. Durchweg ist er dazu verurteilt, die Welt passiv zu erfahren; es ist, als ergreife sie Besitz von ihm, eher als daß er sich ihrer bemächtigen könnte.

Zu dem Eindruck einer den Menschen überwältigenden Erfahrung, der er nicht entrinnen kann, trägt wesentlich auch die Wiedergabe des Geschehens bei. Die Ereignisse vollziehen sich innerhalb einer knappen Woche. Wichtiger aber als der objektiv gegebene zeitliche Rahmen ist abermals das subjektive Empfinden des Jungen. Bezeichnend ist eine zeitliche Verknüpfung wie die folgende: »Get on to bed. We'll be there to-morrow«, sagt Ab Snopes zu seinem Sohn; der nächste Satz lautet: »To-morrow they were there« (S. 12). Es ist, als nähme der Junge die Vorgänge in der vom Vater diktierten Weise wahr. Die Handlung scheint sich unaufhaltsam zu entwickeln, mit der gleichen »machine-like deliberation« (S. 17), die Faulkner den Bewegungen Ab Snopes' zuspricht. Wie sehr sie den Jungen mitreißt, wird besonders am Ende deutlich, wenn sich verschiedene Vorgänge überschneiden, ein zweiter und dritter begonnen hat, ehe der erste abgeschlossen ist. Sarty ist dem Geschehen ausgeliefert, er kann es gerade noch registrieren, aber seinen Verlauf nicht beeinflussen. Er ist, wie es in der bereits zitierten Passage heißt, »[...] just heavy enough to prevent his soaring free of the world as it seemed to be ordered but not heavy enough to keep him footed solid in it, to resist it and try to change the course of its events« (S. 13 f.).

In der Art der Verknüpfung der Ereignisse ist »Barn Burning« typisch sowohl für Faulkners Erzählungen wie für seine Romane. Eine deutlich ausgeprägte Erwartungshaltung, das Gefühl, daß ein Ereignis unmittelbar bevorsteht, und das ängstliche Warten auf das, was die Zukunft birgt, kennzeichnen viele seiner Werke. Sie sind in mancherlei Hinsicht dem Kriminalroman verwandt, der seine Spannung gewöhnlich ja auch aus der Erwartung künftiger Ereignisse bezieht. In dem berühmten Kapitel »The Bear« aus dem Roman *Go Down, Moses* wird die Haltung des Protagonisten Ike McCaslin, der darauf wartet, daß sich ihm die Wildnis offenbart, einmal als »an eagerness, passive«[6] beschrieben – die gleichen Worte ließen sich auf Sarty anwenden. Wie dieser werden Faulkners Helden oft-

---

6 W. Faulkner, *Novels 1942–1954*, hrsg. von Joseph Blotner und Noel Polk, New York: The Library of America, 1994, S. 147.

mals in eine Handlung hineingezogen, deren Sinn eben außerhalb der Reichweite ihres Verständnisses liegt und die sich vollzieht, ohne daß sie etwas dazutun können. Wohl aus diesem Grunde hat der Autor gern Kinder als seine Protagonisten gewählt.

Schließlich ähnelt »Barn Burning« auch darin anderen Werken Faulkners, daß wir Sarty in einer Fülle unterschiedlicher Kontexte sehen – in seiner Familie, in einem bestimmten sozialen Gefüge, in einer von Rassenunterschieden geprägten Welt, in privaten, aber auch in öffentlichen Zusammenhängen. Der letzte Punkt verdient besondere Beachtung. Zwar ist der Konflikt, in dem sich Sarty befindet, in erster Linie ein persönlicher; er betrifft die Auseinandersetzung zwischen Sohn und Vater und Vater und Sohn. Aber wie sich gezeigt hat, ist der Streit zwischen de Spain und Ab Snopes nur vor dem Hintergrund des herrschenden Wirtschaftssystems zu verstehen und insofern von öffentlicher, politischer Bedeutung. Die öffentliche Dimension der Erzählung wird weiterhin in den beiden Gerichtsszenen deutlich, zum einen durch die Person des Friedensrichters, zum anderen durch die Anwesenheit der Zuschauer, die die Verhandlung in beiden Fällen wie eine Art stummer Chor begleiten. Wie oft in Faulkners Werk wechselt der Blick in »Barn Burning« zwischen der privaten, familiären Sphäre und der öffentlichen Welt hin und her. Dabei werden die beiden Bereiche nicht eigentlich gegeneinander ausgespielt; eher scheint es, als wolle Faulkner uns daran erinnern, daß unsere privaten, persönlichen Erfahrungen immer auch einen öffentlichen Bezug haben.

Vielleicht hängt es mit der Vielfältigkeit seiner Sicht auf die Wirklichkeit zusammen, daß Faulkner so oft denselben Stoff mehrfach behandelt hat und wir dadurch manchen seiner Figuren in sehr unterschiedlichen Konstellationen begegnen. Ab Snopes etwa taucht sowohl in dem bereits erwähnten Fragment *Father Abraham* wie in dem Roman *The Unvanquished* auf, und auch die Geschichte der Brandstiftung wird in dem Roman *The Hamlet* in anderer, verkürzter Form noch einmal erzählt. Die vielfachen Verbindungen, die Faulkners Erzählungen und Romane untereinander eingehen können, ihre Offenheit und Variabilität, machen einen besonderen Reiz seines Werkes aus. Es vermittelt dem Leser in der Tat das Gefühl, sich in einem eigenen »Kosmos« zu bewegen, in dem die Begrenzungen und Bedeutungen des einzelnen Textes vielleicht weniger wichtig sind als das Gefüge, das sich aus ihrem Verbund ergibt. Kaum eine andere Erzählung Faulkners ist besser geeignet, einen Einblick in diesen faszinierenden Kosmos zu vermitteln als »Barn Burning«.

Peter Nicolaisen